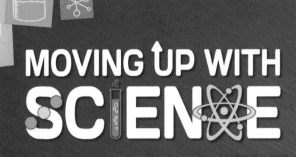

MOVING UP WITH SCIENCE

MATTER

PETER RILEY

PowerKiDS press

To my granddaughter, Holly Jane.

Published in 2017 by
The Rosen Publishing Group, Inc.
29 East 21st Street, New York, NY 10010

Cataloging-in-Publication Data
Names: Riley, Peter.
Title: Matter / Peter Riley.
Description: New York : PowerKids Press, 2017. | Series: Moving up with science | Includes index.
Identifiers: ISBN 9781499431490 (pbk.) | ISBN 9781499431513 (library bound) | ISBN 9781499431506 (6 pack)
Subjects: LCSH: Matter--Properties--Juvenile literature. | Matter--Constitution--Juvenile literature.
Classification: LCC QC173.16 R55 2017 | DDC 530.4--d23

Editor: Hayley Fairhead
Designer: Elaine Wilkinson

Picture credits: Alphaspirit/Dreamstime front cover main; Boule/Shutterstock front cover inset; brackish_nz/ Shutterstock p23b; Chris Bradshaw/Shutterstock p17; Andy Crawford p6, p11t, p11b; i4locl2/ Shutterstock p23t; image.db/Shutterstock p14; Mikko Lemola/Shutterstock p27; Petr Malyshev/ Shutterstock p22; Marafone/Shutterstock p26; Vasiliy Merkushev/ Shutterstock p24–5; Omers/ Shutterstock p7b; pzaxe/Shutterstock p8; shinyshot/Shutterstock p4; Sorbis/Shutterstock p12; stockphoto-graf/Shutterstock title page, p19; Volga/Shutterstock p18.
All other photographs by Leon Hargreaves.

With thanks to our models Sebastian Smith-Beatty, Layomi Obanubi and Sofia Bottomley.

Manufactured in the United States of America
CPSIA Compliance Information: Batch #BW17PK: For Further Information contact Rosen Publishing, New York, New York at 1-800-237-9932.

Contents

Words in **bold** can be found in the glossary on pages 28–29.

Materials

In science, the word **material** is used for anything that contains matter. Matter is simply the "stuff" from which things are made. Scientists divide up materials into three forms, or states of matter, to make them easier to study. The names for the three states of matter are **solids**, **liquids** and **gases**.

Solids and liquids

Solid objects are all around us, such as tables or plates. The liquid we use the most is water. We wash in water, we can feel it as it falls as rain, and we can drink it.

You can find many different solids and liquids when you look around a kitchen. For example, oil and vinegar are liquids; the saucepan and kitchen counter are solids.

Gases

Gases can be found all around us in the form of air. You are surrounded by air and you breathe it in and out. Air is a mixture of gases. You may already know the names of two gases found in the air – oxygen and carbon dioxide.

Helium is a gas that can be used to fill party balloons. Helium is lighter than air which makes the balloons rise up.

List the materials you can see around you and divide them into the three states of matter: solid, liquid, and gas.

Volumes

All matter has **volume**. This is the amount of space that the matter fills. Volume is often measured in units called cubic inches or cubic centimeters.

Solid volume

The volume of a solid block is found by measuring its length, width, and height and then multiplying them all together. For example, if a block is 3 inches long, 2 inches wide, and 1 inch high, its volume is 3 x 2 x 1 = 6 cubic inches.

Use a ruler to measure the length, width, and height of a solid block. Can you now work out its volume?

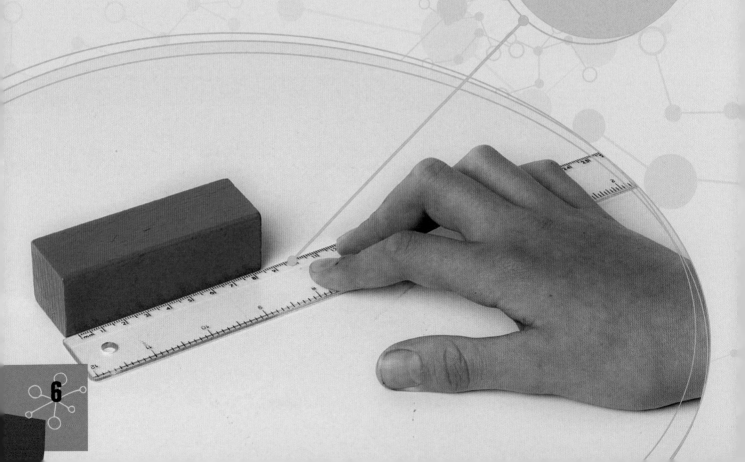

Liquid volume

The volume of a liquid can be found by using a **measuring cylinder** or jug. The liquid is poured in and the mark its surface reaches on the **scale** is the liquid's volume. The scales sometimes used for measuring the volume of a liquid are gallons (gal), liters (l), or milliliters (ml).

Measuring jugs and cylinders have numbered scales on their sides for measuring the volume of a liquid.

As the plunger is pulled out, the gas or liquid enters through the hole in the end of the syringe.

Gas volume

The volume of a gas can be measured in cubic inches, cubic centimeters, or milliliters. A **syringe** can be used to measure the volume of a gas. The scale is on the barrel of the syringe. Syringes can also be used to measure the volume of a liquid.

Make a wall with blocks and try to calculate its volume.

Solids

How can you tell if a material is a solid, liquid, or a gas? Each type of matter has certain features that scientists call **properties**.

Properties of a solid

A solid has a definite shape. Scientists call it a fixed shape. This means that the shape of the solid does not change if you turn it on its side or even upside down. A solid also has a definite volume. It does not change when you try to squash it. Scientists say that a solid cannot be **compressed**.

Sponges or foam

Some solids such as sponges or foam have a fixed shape, but they contain air spaces. When you squeeze them they get smaller because the air is pushed out.

Some solids can be cut and carved into different shapes.

Sand
is a powder.
If you pour a
bucket of dry sand
onto a table, the sand
piles up into a
cone shape.

Powders

Powders are made from many tiny pieces of a solid. Each piece has a definite shape and volume, but when they are put together in large numbers they have another property. If you tip a powder out of its container, it flows. The flowing powder does not splash or form drops like a liquid. When it stops flowing, it forms a cone shape.

Slowly pour half a cup of sugar into a bowl and describe what happens. Can you make the surface of the sugar change by gently shaking the bowl from side to side? Pour a small cup of water into a second bowl and see how a liquid behaves compared to the sugar.

Liquids

How can you tell if a material is a liquid? Liquids flow, but they have other properties too.

Properties of a liquid

A liquid does not have a fixed shape. It takes on the shape of its container. A liquid does have a definite volume, however. It might look like a liquid's volume changes when you pour it from a cup to a saucer, but it actually stays the same.

A liquid cannot be squished. See what happens if you fill a balloon with water and try to squash part of it. The balloon just changes shape as the water inside it moves around.

It may look like the volume of colored liquid in these assorted containers is different, but the same amount of liquid has been poured into each of them.

Pouring liquids

When you pour a liquid very slowly, it forms drops. The drops are round, but become flatter when they land on a surface. When you pour liquid more quickly, it starts to flow. Different liquids flow at different speeds. Thick liquids like honey and bubble bath soap flow slowly, while thinner liquids, such as water and oil, flow much more quickly.

bubble bath soap

water

honey

1.
Compare the flow of each liquid by letting them flow from a line at the top of a plastic tray to a line at the bottom.

cooking oil

top

bottom

2.
Pour each liquid at the same time and start your stopwatch. Time how long each liquid takes to reach the line at the bottom.

Gases

How can you tell if a material is a gas? Most gases do not have any color so we cannot see them.

Properties of a gas

Gases do not have a fixed shape. If you put some gas in a container, it will take on the shape of the container. Gases do not have a fixed volume. If you put a small amount of gas in a large container, it will spread out to fill the whole container. It **expands** to fill the space.

One gas called **neon** shines red when electricity passes through it. Neon can be used to make display signs on shops.

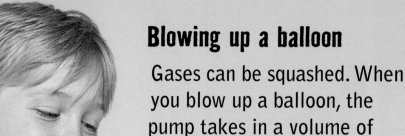

Blowing up a balloon

Gases can be squashed. When you blow up a balloon, the pump takes in a volume of air and squeezed it into the balloon. More and more air is squished into the balloon until it is blown up.

When the balloon cannot hold the volume of air any longer, it will pop!

Stick a ping pong ball to a piece of thread with sticky tape. Hold it up in the wind and photograph it. Take pictures at other times when the wind is blowing. Use the pictures to find out when the wind was strongest.

The flow of gases

Gases flow very easily. The most obvious flow of gas is when air flows as wind, but the flow of air can be produced in hair driers and **air conditioning systems**.

Change and temperature

Materials can change from one state to another. Most of these changes take place when the temperature changes. We measure temperature with a thermometer.

How materials change

A solid can change into a liquid and a liquid can change into a solid. A liquid can also change into a gas and a gas can change into a liquid. These changes can take place if there is a sufficient change in temperature. When ice is heated it turns into water and when water is heated it turns into **steam**.

Perfume is a liquid. When you put perfume on, it is heated up by the skin. This makes the perfume change to a gas, which spreads through the air as a nice smell.

A thermometer

A thermometer is used to find the temperature. It has a scale that measures the temperature in units called degrees, either Fahrenheit (°F) or Celsius (°C). The temperature is found by looking at the top of the column of colored liquid and noting its position on the scale.

The liquid in a thermometer moves up and down as the temperature changes. If it gets warmer, the liquid expands and moves up the scale.

When a thermometer is dipped into a glass of ice, the liquid in the tube **contracts** and moves down the scale to show the low temperature.

How could you record the temperature change as you remove ice cream from a freezer and watch it melt?

Melting and freezing

Melting and **freezing** are two processes that make materials change from one state of matter to another.

Solid to a liquid

When some solids are heated up to a certain temperature, they start to change state. A solid goes soft and loses its fixed shape, then flows away. When this happens, the solid has melted and turned into a liquid. The temperature at which a solid turns into a liquid is called the melting point. Different solids have different melting points. For example, the melting point of butter is between 89.6–95° F (32–35°C), the melting point of chocolate is about 91° F (33°C) and the melting point of a soda can is 1,220° F (660°C).

The chocolate in the bowl has been heated up until it melts. This bar of chocolate has not been heated, so it is still solid.

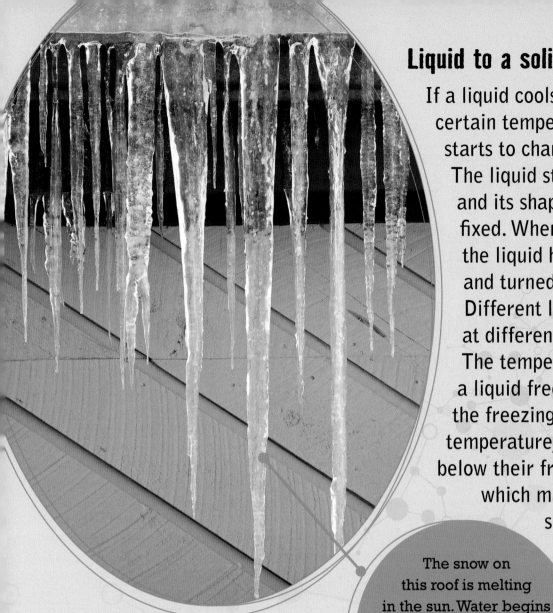

Liquid to a solid

If a liquid cools down to a certain temperature, it also starts to change state. The liquid stops flowing and its shape becomes fixed. When this happens the liquid has frozen and turned into a solid. Different liquids freeze at different temperatures. The temperature at which a liquid freezes is called the freezing point. At room temperature, all metals are below their freezing points which makes them solid, except mercury, which is liquid.

The snow on this roof is melting in the sun. Water begins to drip down, but as the air cools overnight the dripping water becomes solid ice and forms icicles.

Melting and freezing points

The melting and freezing points of a material are the same. When water is cooled to 32° F (0° C) it freezes and turns into the solid form we call ice. The freezing point of water is therefore 32° F (0° C). If ice is warmed up to 32° F (0° C), it melts and turns back into the liquid form of water. The melting point of ice is also 32° F (0° C).

The melting point of tin is 449.6°F (232°C). What is its freezing point?

Evaporation and condensation

Have you noticed how puddles dry up after a rain shower? They slowly get smaller and smaller until they eventually disappear. The water in the puddles warms up in the hot sun and turns into a gas called **water vapor**. This change is due to a process called **evaporation**.

Speed of evaporation

If the air is still, the water vapor stays close to the liquid's surface and stops more water from evaporating. If the wind is blowing, it takes water vapor away from the surface and more liquid water can evaporate. Heat speeds up evaporation; the warmer the day the faster the rate of evaporation.

The heat from the sun is making the water in these puddles evaporate.

The water vapor surrounding these cans has cooled down and formed drops of water.

? What kind of weather do you need to dry a line of wet clothes quickly?

Gas to a liquid

Inside your body, water evaporates from the warm, moist surface of your lungs and forms water vapor. You release it into the air when you breathe out. If you breathe on a cold window, the water vapor changes back to a liquid again and you see it as **droplets**. This process is called **condensation**. It occurs when water vapor cools down.

Measuring changes

You can measure changes in matter, such as melting and evaporation, with the following experiments.

Melting experiment

Compare how fast ice cubes melt at different temperatures using a stopwatch and a thermometer.

Put the ice cubes on a plate and place it in the fridge. Measure the temperature of the air inside the fridge using the thermometer and time how long it takes for the ice cubes to melt. Now try doing this experiment on a sunny windowsill.

Evaporation experiment

Evaporation takes place at the surface of water. You can measure how fast the water evaporates in the following way.

1.
Pour a small amount of colored water onto a plate to make a "puddle" and mark the edge of the puddle with a felt tip pen. Take the temperature of the air and note the time on your watch.

2.
Time how long it takes for you to see that the "puddle" has shrunk away from your original mark due to evaporation. You may have to leave the dish for a few hours or even a day to see this change.

Set up shallow dishes of colored water on a windowsill and in a fridge and record the temperature of the air around them. Which dish of water will evaporate the quickest? Check if your prediction is right when you finish your experiment.

21

Boiling

As water gets warmer, evaporation speeds up and more water vapor escapes from its surface. At 212° F (100° C) a gas called steam forms bubbles in the water and we say that the water is **boiling**. The temperature at which a liquid boils is called its boiling point.

Steam

Steam rises just above boiling water. Steam is a colorless gas so you cannot see it. A couple of inches away from a saucepan of boiling water the temperature falls below 212° F (100° C). The steam condenses to form a white mist of tiny water droplets in the air.

You can clearly see the bubbles of steam inside this glass kettle as the water boils. The bubbles rise up to the surface of the water and pop, releasing steam into the air.

Steam trains

In a steam locomotive water is boiled to make steam. The steam is used to push on pistons to drive the locomotive's wheels. Pistons are discs or tubes which move inside a cylinder. When steam is pushed into the cylinder the piston moves.

The white cloud above this locomotive's funnel is made of water droplets that form when the steam condenses.

Pistons are attached to rods, which move the locomotive's wheels.

What is the difference between water vapor and steam?

The water cycle

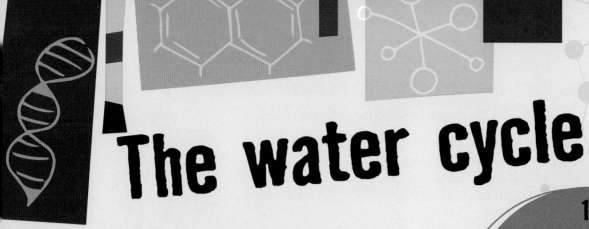

The water on the Earth keeps changing from liquid to gas and then back to a liquid again. These changes form the **water cycle**.

1.
Winds blow clouds made from billions of water droplets over the land. When they reach hills and mountains they rise higher and cool. The water droplets freeze on dust in the air, forming snowflakes.

2.
Snowflakes fall through the cloud, melt, and form raindrops, which fall to the ground. Sometimes, if the air is very cold, the snowflakes fall to the ground without melting.

3.
The rain drains into soil. Some is taken up by plant roots and passes back into the air through their leaves in a process called **transpiration**. This water vapor rises to form clouds again. The rest of the water passes through the soil to streams, then rivers which flow into the seas and oceans.

Storing water

We store water in **reservoirs**, then clean it for people to use. It eventually passes through a wastewater treatment plant and returns to rivers and the sea.

4.
The seas and oceans cover nearly three quarters of the planet. Heat from the sun causes huge amounts of water to evaporate from them every day.

5.
Water vapor rises through the air and cools as it moves away from the warm surface of Earth. Eventually the water vapor gets so cold it condenses on dust in the air to form billions of water droplets. The droplets form clouds and the cycle begins again.

Imagine you are a raindrop. Explain what might happen to you when you reach the ground.

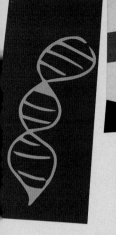

A weather station

The movement of air and water in the water cycle affects our **weather**. Scientists study these movements so they can make **weather forecasts**.

Collecting data

Scientists use the **data** they collect from weather stations like this one to make their predictions. Maps are made to tell people what weather to expect in the next few days.

An anemometer measures the speed of the wind.

A wind vane records the direction from which the wind is blowing.

A thermometer is used to measure air temperature. It is protected from the hot rays of the sun by a screen.

A rain gauge collects and measures the amount of rain that falls from the clouds.

A barometer measures the way the air pushes down on the Earth. This is called air pressure. Changes in air pressure make the winds blow.

Weather maps show people what weather is expected around the world.

Measuring wind speed

You can measure wind speed by looking at the movement of objects, such as trees, outside.

Watch a weather forecast and see how the forecaster talks about wind, rain and temperature. If your school has a weather station, record the weather for a few days and then present a report.

Name of air movement	Things that happen	Wind Speed mph (km/h)
Calm	Nothing moves	<1
Light air	Smoke moves	1–3 (1–5)
Light breeze	Leaves occasionally move	4–7 (6–11)
Gentle breeze	Leaves and twigs move all the time	8–12 (12–19)
Moderate breeze	Small branches move	13–18 (20–28)
Fresh breeze	Small leafy trees sway	19–24 (29–38)
Strong breeze	Large branches move	25–31 (39–49)
High wind (near gale)	All parts of large trees move	32–38 (50–61)
Gale	Twigs broken off branches	39–46 (62–74)

27

Glossary

Air conditioning system a device that cools the air.

Boiling the heating process in which a liquid gets so hot it turns into a gas.

Compress a process in which something is squashed together to make it smaller.

Condensation when a gas changes to a liquid

Contract decrease in volume.

Data a collection of observations and measurements made during an experiment.

Droplet a very tiny drop.

Evaporation When a liquid changes to a gas at a temperature below its boiling point.

Expand increase in volume.

Freezing the process changing from a liquid to a solid.

Gas a material which has no fixed shape or volume. It flows and can be squeezed.

Liquid a material that has a fixed volume and can flow, but does not have a fixed shape and cannot be squeezed.

Material anything that contains matter in one of its three states: solid, liquid, or gas.

Measuring cylinder a container with a scale used for measuring the volume of a liquid.

Melting the process changing from a solid to a liquid.

Neon a gas that is found in very small amounts in the air which glows red when electricity passes through it.

Properties the features of a state of matter, such as a solid's fixed shape or a liquid's ability to flow.

Reservoirs a large lake used to supply homes and other buildings with water.

Scale a series of lines set at a certain distance from each other, which can be used to measure length, volume, and temperature.

Solid a material which has a fixed shape and volume and cannot be squeezed.

Steam the gas form of water at a temperature of 212°F (100°C).

Syringe a hollow cylinder with a sliding plunger at one end and a small hole at the other end. Used to measure the volume of gases or liquids.

Transpiration the escape of water vapor from the surface of a plant.

Volume the amount of space filled by a solid, liquid or a gas.

Water cycle the constant movement of water between the seas and oceans, the air, and the land.

Water vapor the gas form of water at a temperature below 212°F (100°C).

Weather the conditions in the air such as the temperature, wind speed, and amount of cloud cover.

Weather forecast the prediction of future weather conditions for an area.

Answers to the activities and questions

Page 5 Materials

Answer: Solid materials can be described in the objects they form. For example, a plastic straw or a shoe made out of cloth and rubber. Liquids can be specifically named, such as water or olive oil, and also in more general terms, such as shampoo. Air is a mixture of gases all around us. There are also gases in aerosol sprays, such as hairspray.

Page 7 Volumes

Activity: Remember to use a ruler to measure the length, width and height of your wall to calculate the volume.

Page 9 Solids

Activity: The sugar should form a cone. When you shake the plate from side to side, the cone breaks down and the surface of the sugar becomes level. The water will move from side to side with the bowl, but the surface stays level.

Page 13 Gases

Activity: You could ask a friend to take the photographs. The ping pong ball will move away from the wind and tilt the thread when the wind blows. The stronger the wind, the further the ball will tilt.

Page 15 Change and temperature

Answer: Put the bulb of the thermometer in the ice cream as you take it from the freezer and record the temperature shown by the height of the liquid in the scale. Record the temperature every few minutes until the ice cream has completely melted and formed a liquid.

Page 17 Melting and freezing

Answer: 449° F (232° C) (the melting point and the freezing point are the same.)

Page 19 Evaporation and condensation

Answer: A warm, windy day, because evaporation speeds up when it is warmer and moving air carries away water vapor so more can evaporate. The question is about testing knowledge of evaporation, but you might also say it should not be raining!

Page 21 Measuring changes

Activity: The ice cubes will melt more slowly and the water will evaporate more slowly in the cooler temperatures.

Page 23 Boiling

Answer: Water vapor is a gas form of water below its boiling point. Steam is a gas form of water at its boiling point.

Page 25 The water cycle

Answer: There are many possible answers. Here are two examples:

1. You could go into the ground, into a plant root and out through the plant's leaves into the air as water vapor, then rise up, cool down and turn into a water droplet in a cloud.

2. You could flow down a stream, then down a river, and out into the sea where you evaporate from the surface to form water vapor. You would rise up as water vapor, cool down and turn into a water droplet in a cloud.

Page 27 A weather station

Activity: It is important to be able to talk about scientific facts to people. This is what a weather presenter does in a weather forecast. Look at the weather now and describe it to someone. If your school has a weather station, find the temperature, the direction of the wind, its strength and how much rain has fallen. This data will help you write your report about the weather during the last few days.

Index